LOVEBIRDS

Esther Verhoef

# LOVEBIRDS

REBO
PUBLISHERS

© 2002 Zuid Boekprodukties
© 2006 Rebo Publishers

Text: Esther Verhoef
Photographs: Pieter van den Hooven e. a.
Cover design: Astron studio, Prague, The Czech Republic
Typesetting and pre-press services: Artedit s.r.o., Prague, The Czech Republic

ISBN 13: 978-90-366-1550-1
ISBN 10: 90-366-1550-X

# CONTENTS

# 1 THE DIFFERENT TYPES

## Love-Having Bird

The name *agapornis* is the Latin name for the species commonly known as lovebirds. It is a compound name originating from ancient Greek. The ancient Greek word *agapein* means love-having and the word *ornis* means "bird." The meaning of this word then, when freely translated, is "love-having bird," or, put more simply, "lovebird." In English speaking countries, the animals are commonly known as "lovebirds." The name comes from the fact that once lovebirds have formed a pair, they stay faithful to each

> Lovebirds live, on average, for 12 to 15 years. There are reports of birds that have lived for 2 or 3 years longer, but these are exceptions.

other. As soon as one of the pair dies, the surviving partner will form a bond with another.

## What is a Lovebird?

Lovebirds, also known as agapornis, are a group of nine different types of small African parrot species. What the group has in common on the outside is a strong, sturdy body, a large beak and head, and a relatively short tail. Their length, measured from the top of the head to the end of the tail, is somewhere between 5 and 7 inches. The best known, and most kept, are the types commonly known as the *Fischeri* (Fischer's Lovebird), the *Rosiecollis* (Peach-faced Lovebird), and the *Personatus* (Yellow-collared Lovebird).

## *Agapornis canus*

The *Agapornis canus* is often shortened to *Canus* or *Cana*, and is commonly known as the Gray-headed Lovebird, Lavender-headed Lovebird, or Madagascar Lovebird. This small type measures approximately 5 to 6 inches. The *Cana* comes from wooded areas on the island of the Madagascar, and has spread to surrounding islands off the east coast of Africa. There is a recognized sub-

Agapornis canus,
*female*

species, known by the name *A. canus ablectanea*. This is distinguished from the nominate form by its color – the subspecies is darker. The Cana is one of the few types of lovebird where the difference between male and female animals can be seen from its color; male animals have a mouse-gray head and neck, while the females are predominantly green. When these birds are not living as a pair, they live in large groups. In the mating season, however, the formed pairs split themselves off from the group to make a nest. They mainly eat rice in their natural habitat. The *Cana* are, relatively speaking, not often kept by hobbyists. This is possibly because of breeding results. They do not reproduce as easily in cages or aviaries as the more popular lovebird species. Just like the *pullarius* (Red-faced Lovebird), this type is much calmer and more diffident than most of the other lovebirds. They are also quite shy and reserved. That means that it's better not to keep them together with other, more aggressive lovebirds. You can keep a group of Cana together in an aviary as long as you take into account that the birds can be very ill-mannered to each other during mating season. During this time, separate accomodation in pairs is the recommended way to keep the birds. The *Cana* originate from wooded areas, and it appears that they also prefer to have lots of green food in their aviary. A well-planted, spacious aviary in a calm place is, therefore, ideal for them.

## Agapornis fischeri

This type measures approximately 5 to 6 inches, and belongs to the group of four lovebird types with a white ring around the eye (white periopthalmic ring), the personatus group. It is one of the most popular types of lovebird, not only in aviaries with breeders, but also for keeping as a caged bird. The *Fischeri* takes its name from its discoverer, Dr. Fischer, who first described the birds in 1887. This type is sometimes also given the popular name *Fischer's* Lovebird, but most hobbyists refer to it with its generic name Fischeri. It grows to approximately 6 inches long. The natural habitat of the *Fischeri* is (the north of) Tanzania. The animals live there in a dry environment, in small groups. They eat mainly (grass) seeds. There is no difference in appearance between the two sexes. The *Fischeri* can crossbreed with types belonging to the personatus group. Even though such cross breeding is sometimes undertaken, it is generally not recommended because it does not serve any real purpose. Most hobbyists

Agapornis fischeri,
*pastel olive green*

**Agapornis fischeri, *natural***

**Fischeris, *left: violet* *right: cobalt blue***

are strongly in favor of keeping every race of lovebird pure. Also, because of their large capacity for adapting to change, and their relatively simple breeding, there are countless color mutations. Mutations that the species has brought about itself include the very well known edged and piebald color varieties (including recessive, dominant as well as mottled types), and possibly also the Yellow-collared Lovebird. Other successful color combinations, such as the blue, violet and darker forms, have been "borrowed" from the *Personatus*. The ino strain (with red eyes) was brought in to the race through crossbreeding with the *Lilianae*. In the wild, the birds like to nest in tree hollows, but if these can't be found, it appears that animals bred in captivity aren't very choosy when it comes to finding an alternative nesting place. The

**Agapornis fischeri, *lutino***

**Agapornis fischeri, *pastel sky blue***

Fischeri make a nest from raw materials such as twigs and small sticks. Three to five small white eggs are laid that the female broods. She does this, on average, for about 20 days before they hatch. Young animals are recognizable from the black on the base of their beak. They often also have a red dot on their beak. You can keep these birds as a pair, but keeping them together in small groups is also possible. Even though there is a good chance of discord within the group, this is not a problem in a large aviary. It is better to keep formed pairs accommodated separately during the breeding season. Alongside the natural, wild, color combinations, there have been very many other color mutations developed and reported, such as the very common light green and sky blue Fischeri, that haven't been combined with pastel strains. Lutino (yellow with red eyes) and albino (white with red eyes) mutations can also be found.

## Agapornis lilianae

The *Lilianae* (pronounced liliarnay) belongs to the personatus group. This is a group of four different types that have a white ring around the eye. This type is also called the Nyasa Lovebird, or Lilian's Lovebird, but most hobbyists simply call them Lilianae. Lilianae can be found in Zambia, Tanzania, and Zimbabwe, where they keep themselves in large groups ("colonies"), mainly in wetland areas. Even though this type had already been discovered and described as early as 1864, and taken to Europe about half a century later, hobbyists keep them in much fewer numbers than the Fischeri and the Personatus. It's the smallest type of lovebird known to us –

Agapornis lilianae

Agapornis lilianae, *lutino*

adult animals measure approximately just 5 inches. There is no difference in appearance between the sexes. The Lilianae has two color strains. The original wild color, and the lutino. The latter is a mainly yellow colored bird, with red eyes, that is not often seen. This type is known for having a gentle nature, and it can be kept with other birds either of the same type, or with other, smaller birds, generally without problems. They prefer to breed in small groups.

## Agapornis nigrigenis

The *Agapornis nigrigenis* belong together with the Fischeri, Lilianae and Personatus in the personatus group. They are lovebirds with a white ring around the eye. The popular name for this type is the Black-cheeked Lovebird (or Black-faced Lovebird), but hobbyists usually call this type by its gender name – *Nigrigenis*. The Nigrigenis can crossbreed with other strains that belong to the personatus group. Even though breeders have often made use of this, with the intention of introducing new colors, the cross breeding of different types is generally discouraged as it is more and more evident that it is better to keep separate races pure. That is definitely the case with this bird, as it is recognized as an endangered species in its native country. The Nigrigenis comes from Zambia, where it was discovered by Kirkman in 1904. They live in groups, in places where woodland, wetland, and dry, open spaces are close to each other. They eat mainly different types of seed. With a body measuring about 5 inches, the Nigrigenis is one of the smaller lovebirds. Even though they are seldom found in the wild,

Agapornis
nigrigenis,
*natural coloring*

Agapornis
nigrigenis,
*light green
washed*

Agapornis
nigrigenis,
*cobalt blue*

they are well represented in hobbyist circles. Several diverse mutations are known. In all probability, just two of these types occur naturally. The other color mutations have come about through crossbreeding with other types. The race mutations consist of the pale, washed, and blue strains. In all probability the inos and the darker varieties came about through cross breeding. The Nigrigenis has one of the gentlest natures of all lovebirds. It is very possible to keep several couples together in an aviary. The aviary, however, must be big enough, and the owner must always keep an eye on them so that they can intervene should something appear to be going wrong. Just like all four types from the personatus group, there are no differences in appearance between the two sexes.

## Agapornis personatus

The *Agapornis personatus*, approximately 6 inches long, is better known as the Personatus, or the Yellow-collared Lovebird (or the Masked Lovebird, the Black-masked Lovebird, the Black-faced Lovebird, or the Black-headed Lovebird). It originates

Agapornis personatus, *natural coloring*

Agapornis personatus, *albino*

Agapornis personatus, *from left to right: cobalt blue, violet and sky blue*

from Tanzania where its living environment is mainly restricted to the Irangi district in the northeast of the country. It has a very dark brown to black head, and contrasting white ring around the eye. It was discovered and described in 1887. The Yellow-collared Lovebird is very popular, and is often kept as a caged or show bird. In its natural environment, it prefers to breed in tree hollows, but in aviaries they appear to be much less particular when choosing a nesting place. Even though they live in groups in the wild, and can be kept in groups in aviaries, it's better to accommodate them separately as couples during the mating season. A nest is made from all types of raw materials, and 3 to 4 eggs, on

average, are laid. After about 45 days, the young ones leave the nest. There have been many reported color mutations over a period of time. Of these, the (Dutch) blue mutation is the most original and loved. Dark, pastel, violet and fallow (pale brownish or reddish yellow) strains also exist. The ino strain (with red eyes) has been "borrowed" from the Lilianae, while the Fischeri accounts for the multicolored strains. The Yellow-Collared Lovebird belongs to the group of lovebirds with a white ring around the eye, the "personatus group." The animals in this group can crossbreed easily. Even though crossbreeding with other types is done quite often, most hobbyists are of the opinion that this crossbreeding of wild colors should be kept to a minimum, so as to keep the races pure. Just like most other lovebirds, there is no difference in appearance between the male and female animals.

## Agapornis pullarius

Also well known by the popular name Red-faced Lovebird (or Red-headed Lovebird), or, in hobbyist circles, simply Pullaria, this type is calmer than most other lovebirds, and doesn't fly much, relatively speaking, though it does climb and crawl more. The Pullaria appears in the wild in the west of central Africa, in Togo, Sierra Leone and Ghana, amongst other places. There is a known sub-species, that is only found in Uganda and neighboring areas, known as *A. pullarius*

Agapornis
pullarius,
*male*

An Agapornis
pullarius,
*couple*

*ugandae*. Pullarias are widely believed to be the first type of
lovebird to have appeared in Europe. It is believed that the
Portuguese took them out of Africa in the sixteenth century. Nowadays this type is only found relatively rarely with
hobbyists. With the Pullaria, the differences in appearance
between males and females are visible. The male animals
are recognizable from their blue wing edges. Furthermore,
the males have a clear red coloring, where the females have
more of an orange tint on the neck, cheeks, and top of the
head. Both sexes have a blue tail. The Red-faced Lovebird
is approximately 6 inches long, measured from the end of
the tail to the top of the skull. In the wild, this type lives in
large groups, where they look for large open spaces so that
they can feed themselves on their diet of mainly all kinds of
grass seeds. In a large aviary, it is better to keep the animals

together with other couples of the same type, than to keep
them as a single couple. Thanks to their relatively peaceful
nature, keeping them together with other types of lovebirds is not recommended–other types are mostly more
aggressive and prone to fighting, so the Pullaria could
come off worst. The Pullaria also differs with other lovebirds regarding their nesting place. They only breed in termite hills and in termite nests that are found high up in the
trees. The female makes a nesting place with an entrance
in such a termite hill. The newly born young are also different from other types of lovebird in that they are not covered in down, but are completely bald. The down only
starts to appear after a few days. This type is relatively seldom kept by hobbyists because of the fact that breeding in
captivity is very rarely successful.

---

The term dimorphic ("two forms") is used for types of lovebird where
there are obvious differences in appearance between the male and female
animals. There are three types of dimorphic lovebird, namely the Agapornis
pullarius, the Agapornis taranta and the Agapornis canus.

---

## Agapornis roseicollis
This is the most adored and recognizable lovebird, also
commonly known by the name of Peach-faced Lovebird, or

Rosiecollis. If people who are not breeders are talking about lovebirds, they usually mean this type. There is a known sub-species that can be found in Angola. The Latin name for this type is *Agapornis roseicollis catumbella*. The sub-species is a bit smaller than the nominate type, and it has a lighter colored beak. The Peach-faced Lovebird originates from south-west Africa where it lives in drier areas. The Rosiecollis lives on a diet of (grass) seeds and small berries, depending on the season. These lovebirds are extremely sociable. As young animals, they live in enormous flocks. When they become adult, they split off into smaller groups. They can be kept together with several couples in an aviary, but the chance remains that the couples will, during the mating season, form partnerships that last for life. That's why most breeders choose to accommodate the birds as couples. This, in any case, is not only because of the aggression that can arise between the couples themselves, but also because this is the only way to keep a close eye on the correct breeding for certain color combinations. Peach-faced Lovebirds are not active nest builders. They breed in the wild mainly in hollow trees, which they cover with twigs and husks. The females stuff the gathered nest materials between their feathers and transport them in this manner to the nest. It also appears that this type regularly steals weaverbirds' nests, and that they, in such a case, seldom make an effort to decorate the nest any further. Because this

*Agapornis roseicollis, natural coloring*

*Agapornis roseicollis, pale-masked violet*

type is very often kept also by breeders, and they are relatively easy to breed, there are very many recognized color mutations. The Rosiecollis exists in a wild color, also known as light green, and also in dark green, olive green, sea green, opal, lutino, pale-masked, peach-masked, orange-masked, multicolored pastel, washed, fallow (pale brownish or reddish-yellow), cinnamon, isabel (grayish yellow), yellow black eye, and in recessive and dominant multicolors. They are approximately 6 inches long, and there are no differences in appearance between the male and female animals.

## Agapornis swindernianus

The approximately 5 inch long *Agapornis swindernianus* (also known as the Black-collared Lovebird, Swinderen's Lovebird, or the Liberian Lovebird) has two sub-species, the *Agapornis swindernianus amini* and the *Agapornis swindernianus zenkeri*. Even though this type was first discovered and described as early as 1820, the nominate type and its sub-species are not known as cage or aviary birds. This is very probably due to the fact that the birds cannot be kept alive in captivity, possible because of too many stress factors or a disability to adapt from their natural diet. This type appears in impenetrable forests in Liberia, and there is very little known about their living habits, or reproduction.

## Agapornis taranta

This brightly colored type of lovebird appears in Ethiopia and some neighboring areas. The popular name is the

Abyssinian lovebird, or Black-winged Lovebird, but many hobbyists simply call them Taranta. They are also sometimes called Mountain Lovebirds or Mountain Parrots, because they originate from mountainous areas. The name Taranta also refers to a mountain range in their home-

**Agapornis swindernianus**

land. Abyssinian Lovebirds are real group birds. They prefer to live in small groups, and feed themselves on all kinds of seeds and berries. The animals grow to approximately 6 or 7 inches long. There is a sub-species that is known by the name *Agapornis taranta nana*. This differs from the nominate type by its shorter wings and smaller beak. The difference between the two sexes can easily be noticed from their coloring. The males are real eye-catchers with their bright red patterning around the eyes and on the forehead. The females do not have this patterning, but they are not outdone in the beauty stakes thanks to the contrast between their green feathers and bright red beak. The females also have a slightly lighter black coloring on the underside of the wings than do the males. This type is widely available and is therefore more common than the other two types from the dimorphic group, the *Agapornis canus* and the *Agapornis pullarius*. Diverse color mutations occur, thanks to breeders. The type doesn't only occur in wild colors ("light green"), but also appears in olive green, dark green, fallow, lutino and cinnamon.

**Agapornis taranta,**
*fallow and natural*
*coloring*

**Agapornis taranta –** *the*
*underside of the wings*
*is darker in male*
*animals*

# 2 PURCHASING

## Is a lovebird appropriate for me?

Lovebirds are nice, pleasant, colorful, sociable, hardy birds, that are easy to care for. Thanks to their big, round eyes, they often give off a lovely, cheerful feeling. Young animals can be very well domesticated and form a strong bond with their owner. It is therefore no wonder that these birds are so popular as pets. You probably already know the advantages of keeping a lovebird as a pet. But keeping these birds does also have its disadvantages. These disadvantages can become more of a problem for many people as time progresses. You should therefore seriously consider the negative aspects before deciding to purchase a lovebird. Some of these are:

### • The sound of their voice

Lovebirds have a very loud and shrill voice, that not everybody appreciates. In the wild they use these calls to stay in contact with other birds of the same type. It will not surprise anybody who knows how loud they can be, that the animals can hear each other over very long distances.

In a room in a house, this same, shrill noise can sometimes cause irritation. If several lovebirds are kept outside in an aviary, they can make such a combined racket that it can lead to problems with other people in the neighborhood. If

*Lovebirds are intelligent and they need lots of activity to feel happy*

you want to keep several lovebirds outside, then it is essential to have good relationships with your neighbors, and possibly even prior discussions with them.

*Agapornis taranta – olive green, light green and dark green*

• **Sociable nature**

A lovebird does not have the instinct necessary to go through life on its own. If a bird is kept on its own, it will want to form a strong bond with its owner. A lovebird can become so attached to its owner that, if its social outlook is neglected, it can literally become sick from loneliness. If you want to tame a single bird, you must realize that the lovebird will view you as its partner. And that the bond

*Lovebirds are very sociable birds that enjoy each other's company*

between you and the animal is not without obligation. Getting rid of the animal because you later realize that it really is too much work, or because it is too loud, would be a very traumatic experience for an animal that is totally dedicated to you. So seriously consider, beforehand, if you think you really will find it so pleasant when you have to give your lovebird at least a few hours of attention every day, for fifteen years or more. Only if you keep a pair of birds is this attention less important. The animals will then have enough company from each other.

• **Extra cleaning**
Lovebirds make considerably more mess than smaller birds such as canaries or budgerigars. The cleaning of the cage, as well as the surrounding area, therefore also always brings extra work with it.

*Left: an*
**A. nigrigenis,**
*right: an*
**A. personatus**

## • Responsibility

When purchasing a lovebird, you are taking home a living animal that is completely dependent on you for its feeding, care, accommodation, and possibly also medical attention. If you already know that you are not prepared to drive miles in order to see a specialized veterinarian, then please do not take on the responsibility that keeping a living and dependent animal brings with it.

## Male or female?

Most people who want one or two lovebirds as a pet will choose the *Agapornis rosiecollis*. This is far and away the most widely kept pet and it does its job exceptionally. Furthermore, it is a type that is relatively cheap to purchase. But it is also one of the types of lovebird where it is difficult to determine the difference between males and females. The owner often only realizes the gender of his or her bird when the bird shows behavior that is typical for one of the genders. It often becomes apparent when female animals, even if they are being kept as a sole pet, go to build a nest in the spring. They can sometimes become extremely aggressive in defending their nest—even towards the owner! Some females lay eggs, even if there are no males in the vicinity. Male animals can, under the influence of hormones, "ride" the perch, other objects, or even people. Apart from this hormonally driven behavior, that they often—but not always—restrict to the spring and summer months, there are actually not really any behavioral

*It is not desirable to keep a lovebird on its own*

*Lovebirds are extremely curious*

differences between the male and female birds that are kept as pets. If you definitely want either a male or a female, or, for example, a couple, then it can be difficult for the breeder to fulfill this wish. However, very experienced breeders can often give an indication as to the gender of adult birds by feeling the pelvic bones. This method, however, is not always watertight. Moreover, the "pelvic test" can only be carried out when the bird is sexually mature, and so at least approximately nine months old. A house bird is often purchased at a much younger age. There are, in fact, even more methods for determin-

*A group of young lovebirds*

ing the gender. You can read more about this in the "Breeding" chapter.

### One or two birds?

Opinion is very strongly divided on whether it is desirable to keep sociable birds, such as lovebirds, on their own. Some people think that a human can never take the place of a partner of the same species, even if this is only because a person, as opposed to a bird of the same type, cannot or does not want to spend twenty-four hours a day with the bird. Other people think that the bird is not really damaged if it has contact, for at least a few hours a day, with its human partner, and is also sufficiently occupied with games. In any case, it is best for the well-being of your birds (and more elegant) that you purchase a couple if you are outside of the house a lot. A couple, whether it really is a "couple," or just two males or females, will receive sufficient company from each other. This is also of course advisable if you would like to breed your birds. Would you just like to have interaction with your bird? Do you have the necessary time to spend? Would you like to have a pet that is totally focused on you? And does the knowledge that your bird will make demands on your time for your attention every day for the next fifteen years not scare you off? Then the choice for a single, preferably young, or hand-reared bird, is a logical one. One option does not necessarily rule out the other. It is very possible to keep several tame birds together. In this case it is better to purchase a bird that is already tame, and introduce another bird thereafter.

*A bird that has been kept on its own for a long time usually sees a newcomer as an intruder*

*Fischeri,*
*Cobalt blue edged*

*Young lovebirds*
*are recognizable*
*for their (partly)*
*black beak*

## Keeping several lovebirds together

If you want to keep a group of lovebirds together, you must take into account that lovebirds which normally get on very well together, can sometimes react very aggressively to types of their own kind, and other birds, during mating season. This is certainly the case for couples, who can become unbearable to other couples or single birds. Supplying them with nesting boxes can promote this aggression, because the animals will want go and claim their own place in the aviary or large cage. So it is better to not give the animals any nesting boxes or "sleeping bags," and be sure to keep an eye on them, definitely in the spring and summer, so that they can be placed separately if it threatens to not go well. Aggression, such as is described here, is seldom a problem with some of the lesser known types of lovebird, such as the *Agapornis lilianae*, the *Agapornis nigrigenis*, and the *Agapornis pullarius*. For

Agapornis
fischeri

instance, the Lilianae and the Pullarius are generally peaceful within a group.

## Introducing a new bird

If you want to keep two lovebirds, it is best to go for two young birds. Young animals usually accept each other quite quickly, and without a problem. On the other hand, older animals, especially if one, or both, of them has spent some time alone, can often find it more difficult to learn how to live with each other. Whatever you do, make sure that you don't make the mistake of suddenly putting a new bird in a cage with an "old" one. A lovebird seldom sees a newcomer as a new friend, but more often as an intruder on its territory. This can lead to all kinds of, sometimes disastrous, consequences. Have you already had a lovebird for a while, and want to introduce a second? Then go about it with the right policies. It is best to purchase a second cage and put the old bird in that. This is because the cage that you already have is your old bird's territory. Now clean this (old) cage thoroughly, and completely redecorate it so that, with the exception of the cage itself, nothing remains the same. This will mean the old bird will no longer recognize its cage as its own territory. Put the newcomer in this cage. Then put both cages

*If you want to start breeding, it's best to look for unrelated animals*

next to each other, so that the animals can see and hear each other, and can get used to each other safely. Depending on how they react with each other, you can let them

*Young that come "straight from the nest" usually become tame very quickly*

out into the room together after a few days or a week. Only when the animals really do seem to be getting on with each other can you put them together in a cage, and so remove the second cage.

## A tame bird

The Rosiecollis is considered to be the easiest bird to tame. And that is why this bird is the most common sort found in a cage. The Fischeri and the Personatus, however, can also

*If a young animal is used to people when you purchase it, it will already be tame*

make exceptional housemates. If it is important for you that the birds become tame, it is best to purchase a very young bird. At an age of six to eight weeks (sometimes longer), young Rosiecollis birds are recognizable from their still (partly) black beak. You can also opt for a hand-reared bird. These are already tame at the time of purchase. However, not all lovebirds are suitable to keep as birds for companionship. The general opinion is that it is better not to keep the rarer types as caged birds. The few birds that there are,

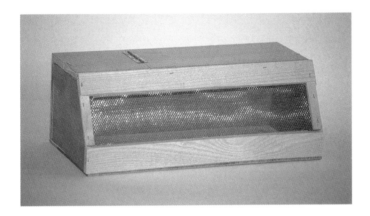

*Traveling box*

are better used for breeding so that they can help to keep the species in existence. Only if it appears that an individual bird is not suitable for this purpose, can its life as a pet be justified.

*A big bird exhibition is a great place to get to know your way around*

# What do I need to look out for?

When you go to a specialist pet shop or a breeder to purchase your animals, you need to look out for a few things. First of all you need to have a good look at the accommodation and surrounding areas of the animals on offer. Does it look hygienic? Have the animals got sufficient water and food available to them, or are their food trays empty? Are the food and water containers clean? Or are they dirty with droppings or crusted dirt? You should also have a good look at the bird droppings on the bottom of the cage. They can give an indication as to the health of the animals. Lovebirds' excrement should never be (too) fluid. On the contrary, it should be quite firm. If that's all okay, have a good look at the birds. A healthy bird is recognizable from various characteristics.

- The feathers are nice and smooth – a lovebird should never have bald patches or feathers that stick out from the body
- There are no traces of excrement or damp patches under the tail—this can be an indication of eating disorders and/or harmful bacteria
- The claws and feet should be clean and smooth
- The feet should be normally formed—toe and nail amputations are often caused by external factors, but if the bird is hindered, it isobulous that it would be better not to purchase it
- The eyes should be big and round, not narrowed, and there should be no trace of weepiness
- Their behavior should be lively and curious, not apathetic
- The beak should be smooth, clean, and the normal shape, with nothing seeping out from the nose holes
- The breastbone should not be obviously visible or too sharp when touched

# What do I need to look out for with bred birds?

Ultimately, the birds that you are planning to use for breeding should come up to the same standards as a bird you would buy as a pet. In fact, because you want to breed the birds, there are some other important factors to consider.

- It is best to look for unrelated, or at least not too closely related, birds to put together. Ask the breeder specifically about this.
- Purchase some birds that have been officially ringed. Only ringed birds are registered so you know that the bird has not come from being captured in the wild. Furthermore, a ring gives you the certainty of knowing what year the animal was born in (you can read more about rings in the "Breeding" chapter).

- Are the birds that you are purchasing the gender that you want? If the breeder has had a gender test carried out on the birds, or if the couple has already successfully mated, then you can be pretty sure. But this is seldom the case in reality. It is therefore best to arrange with the breeder that you can swap (one of) the birds if it later appears not to be of the required gender.
- If you don't have any previous breeding experience, it is best to go for the naturally wild colored animals. Every different colored type of bird has specific qualities and some types are frankly difficult to breed.
- Have a good look beforehand at the importance people give to the bird's body color and build at shows and exhibitions. This basic knowledge is indispensable if you want to purchase good breeding stock.
- It is best to purchase a couple for breeding from a well-known breeder. You can ask for addresses of serious breeders from your national or local association.

## Transporting them home

If you purchase your lovebird from a specialist pet shop, you will usually be given your animal in a small cardboard box, with air holes for ventilation. Such boxes are only intended for short trips because your lovebird will be able to free itself from such housing without too much trouble, using its strong beak, as soon as it gets too scared. If it's a longer trip, then it's better to borrow or purchase a special travel cage. If you are borrowing a cage, first make sure that it has been cleaned with disinfectant, and also make sure that it is cleaned again once you have finished with it, so as to avoid the risk of spreading germs. Transport is, for most lovebirds, their most stressful experience. To keep the stress levels to a minimum, make sure that your bird can see as little as possible. The darker it is, the calmer the birds will be able to keep themselves. You can, for example, put the travel cage in another closed cardboard box into which you have already put holes. Birds are very bad at adjusting to changes in temperature. Try to avoid this as much as possible during transportation. On days that are too hot or extremely cold, do not transport birds–the change can be fatal.

*p. 37:*
Agapornis
nigrigenis, *light
green pastel*

# 3 ACCOMMODATION

## An indoor cage–the bars

There are countless types of lovebird cages for sale. Some are nicer and more colorful than others. What these cages have, or should have, in common, is the thickness of the bars. These must be very strong so as to give the animals no chance of biting through them with their sharp beaks, and escaping. Gauze and thin wires such as are used for small tropical birds cannot withstand the force from a strong lovebird beak. Because the animals like climbing, and can get a better grip on horizontal bars than on vertical ones, it is preferable to purchase a cage with horizontal bars. If you buy a cage with colored bars, take into account the fact that your animals could chew the colored layer off. This is why it is better to get a cage with chrome bars. In any case, take a good look at the distance between the bars. It cannot be more than an inch for a lovebird. Because lovebirds are very good at making a mess, it is also a good idea to put some plexiglass on the inside of the cage up to about half way. Then put the water and food trays low down, so the seed husks and other bits do not fall out of the cage. There are some cages that come ready-made from the factory with plexiglass already fitted. It is best not to choose a cage that

*A popular type of indoor cage for lovebirds*

*Wooden cages need to be well maintained and must be changed when necessary for hygiene*

is predominantly made from plexiglass, as the temperature in such a cage can become very high and, moreover, there is little ventilation, and this can lead to health problems for the bird.

## An indoor cage–the size

A cage can never be too big. Lovebirds are very mobile and they need space. If your bird rarely or never comes out of its cage, then the cage must definitely be on the large side, at least 25 inches across. It is more important to have a wide cage than a high cage. A high cage does not

*A cage can never be too big*

give the animal much of a chance to spread its wings. If you have enough room and your budget permits, consider purchasing a room aviary, where your bird will have lots of space.

## An indoor cage–the location
Your cage should deserve its own permanent place in the house. This is because constantly moving the cage is confusing for the bird. Its standing place cannot be in direct sunlight, not even for a couple of hours a day, but a dark corner is just as bad a place. A bit of morning sun is very

*If you have sufficient space, a room aviary is always a better choice than an indoor cage*

welcome. Most birds like to have a good view, and can become anxious when their view becomes obscured. That's why it's best to put the cage up high somewhere. Lovebirds are, just like all birds, extremely sensitive to damp conditions. Make sure their standing place is free from damp, even if windows and doors are open. It would also be good if the chosen place is sheltered, such as in a location next to a wall. The (dining) kitchen is not a good place to put a cage. There can sometimes be fumes in the kitchen that can be extremely poisonous for birds. For example, Teflon non-stick pans or ovens can give off poisonous gasses if they become too hot (read more about this in the "Illnesses" chapter).

A **Rosiecollis** *in a special "lovebird tent"*

## An indoor cage–the perches

Some lovebird cages come ready-made with perches. They are often not really suitable perches–they are made of plastic, are too thin, and have the same diameter all the way along. Plastic perches are easy to clean, and so hygienic, but they do not give a bird enough of a grip, and this can easily wear the birds' claws out. Wooden perches are therefore a

*It's best for lovebirds to have a variety of perches with differing diameters*

better choice. Lovebirds like to gnaw on their perches. You can just let them get on with it, and replace the old perches with new ones when necessary. But you could also choose to purchase hardwood perches that can resist their strong beaks better. Whatever you do, make sure you choose perches of differing thicknesses. In this way, the bird is not forced to always put his claws in the same position when grabbing the perch. That can be annoying for the bird, and can also cause painful wounds. You can choose to make your own perches from twigs and sticks from fruit trees and willows. These look very natural, are cheap, and they give the bird more grip. Lovebirds like having normal twigs as something to gnaw on. If you want to use natural sticks as perches, make sure that the trees that they come from have not been sprayed, and fasten them securely. You can

*A cross between an* Agapornis rosiecollis *and an* Agapornis fischeri

buy special holders for them. If certain sticks become partly chewed through, after a few weeks, you can simply swap them for new ones. If you want to store some sticks, it is best to do so by keeping them in a dark, cool, dry place, or even in the freezer. Mold and fungus or such like will therefore have less chance of spreading. As well as perches, you can also consider hanging one or more ropes across the birdcage. It is best to use ropes that are sold as toys for lovebirds in specialist pet shops, as these do not contain any poisonous materials.

### An indoor cage–food and drink trays

There are all kinds of food and drink trays for sale, but not all types are suitable for lovebirds. The strongest and most hygienic are those made from stainless steel that you can hang up with a bracket in the cage. Plastic trays, especially the softer types, often get cut up. There are plastic bottles with a reservoir available, for water, as well as for food. These can be hung on the outside of the cage, so that only

*Plastic bottles with a reservoir are often used*

*Purchasing a
birdbath can
sometimes be
unnecessary for
very tame birds!*

the part that a bird eats or drinks from sticks into the cage.
If your lovebird also ruins this, then it's best to go for a
stainless steel one with strong brackets for hanging it up.
Glazed pottery, or porcelain trays, can also make very good
food and water trays. They must be attached high up
because trays that are on the ground can become dirty, with
droppings and such very quickly.

## An indoor cage – a birdbath

Most lovebirds love bathing. It is good for their feather coat
and general health. You can buy ready-made bathing hous-
es that you can hang at an entrance to the cage, but they are
not always appropriate for lovebirds. Certainly, if the fas-
tening leaves something to be desired, an average lovebird
will make light work of pushing the bath to one side, and
making an escape. If you purchase a birdbath that you can
fasten to the cage, make sure that the bath is big enough
and, most of all, that it can be fastened securely. In practice,
it seems that a glazed pottery dish filled with fresh water
and placed on the bottom of the cage still makes the best
bath. Some tame lovebirds prefer taking a shower to taking
a bath–they will fly with you to the sink and wait until you
turn the tap on a little bit. You may also prefer to spray
your bird daily, from a suitable distance, with a plant
sprayer.

Fischeri,
*light green
multicolored*

## An indoor cage–the bottom pan

There are various different ways of covering the bottom
pan. The most commonly used way is with classic bird
sand. You can also cover the bottom with wood chippings. Much less commonly used, and relatively un-
known, are paper coverings. The different types of bottom covering have all got their advantages and
disadvantages. Wood chippings are less dusty than bird
sand, for example. Lots of breeders and hobbyists find
this type of covering less of a problem for the birds' air-
ways. The disadvantage of wood chippings is that they
make a less comfortable floor for lovebirds' sensitive feet
and claws. Paper coverings have the disadvantage that the
animals will sometimes shred them to pieces. But if the
paper is changed twice a week, it does make a very
hygienic covering that is also easy to use. Normal (news)
paper is also much cheaper, but it is better not to use it

*An aviary with different compartments for every type of bird*

because of the ink. If you give your lovebird wood chippings or paper as the bottom covering, make sure that it has access to some sand or gravel in a separate tray–it needs this for optimal digestion.

## An aviary

Keeping lovebirds in an aviary has advantages and disadvantages. One of the disadvantages is that the birds will never form a strong bond with you. This can only be achieved if the birds are kept in the house where they get lots of attention. Another disadvantage of the outdoor accommodation is that your birds can become infected with worms or other illnesses that they can catch from wild birds or mice. To reduce the risk of infection from wild birds, it's best to cover the top of the aviary.

A third disadvantage of keeping lovebirds in an outside aviary is that it's possible that your neighbors will complain about the shrill, loud noises that your birds make. In contrast though, there are also lots of advantages. An average aviary offers a lot more room than can be given inside. The effect of sunlight, the seasons, and the fresh air are all a healthy influence for molting and reproduction.

### An aviary – What do I need to look out for?

If you are building an aviary, or having one built, take the following into account:

- Cover the top so that no excrement from wild birds can fall in (risk of infection). You can use see-through corrugated sheets that will give sufficient light for this.
- Make sure the cover is sloping so that rainwater can run off easily.
- Make sure the aviary has an entrance door that is high enough for you to get through easily.
- Put the aviary in a warm, sheltered place, preferably with the front facing the southeast or southwest.
- Make a night shelter that is easy for both you and the birds to reach.
- Make sure the aviary is easy to clean and disinfect.
- To reduce the risk of escape, a double door (a sluice) is ideal.

### Materials for an aviary

The beaks of a lovebird are notoriously strong, so the aviary must therefore be built from strong materials. Use a hard wood, and cover the wooden bits that the birds can reach with their beak, with metal strips. Do not use gauze. Use strong panels that have been specially made for lovebirds. You can sometimes order these from a well-stocked specialist pet shop, or you can find suppliers' addresses from bird, or bird club, magazines. The width of the mesh should preferably not be more than 0.2 square inches. Put the aviary on a prepared, stone floor. Putting wooden parts directly onto the ground can lead to rotting. This will obviously mean you won't be able to enjoy your aviary for as long. When the aviary is ready, check all corners and gaps very carefully. Look out for thorns, splinters, protruding nails and screws, or loose metal wires that could all wound your birds. Subsequently, you can give the wooden parts a final covering with a lacquer that is harmless for the birds. Only when the smell of paint or lacquer and its particles have fully dissipated can the aviary be used.

## The night or inside compartment

A night compartment protects the birds from freezing cold and other weather. It is best to build it from stone, though good quality hard wood can also be used. It must, however, be draught proof, meaning that it cannot have any holes, gaps, or slits in it. Lovebirds like to make use of nesting boxes to sleep in and also, of course, to nest in. Hang several of these various compartments up in the night compartment, but make sure you keep them all at the same height. A number of sturdy perches, preferably of differing thicknesses so that the birds have a choice, are also a standard part of equipment in a night compartments. The bottom of an internal compartment needs to be easy to clean and disinfect. Concrete is the most hygienic solution, but paving stones or tiles can also be used. Cover the bottom with a thick layer of sand or wood chippings, so that droppings do not go directly onto the floor. Make a raised entrance for the birds so that they can pass between the inside and outside compartments. That will make it easy for them to come in and go out. Make sure that the passageway can be closed off with a sliding door.

## Fresh air or draught?

Birds benefit greatly from fresh air. Nothing is worse for their health than a stuffy, muggy environment. That's why it makes sense to make sure that the place you keep your birds is well-ventilated. But the space mustn't be so well ventilated that there's a draught, because a draught can be disastrous for birds. Also, make sure that you never open two opposing doors or windows that the birds can sit between. They will then be sitting in the draught and that can have deadly consequences. If you need to build a separate inside compartment in the aviary, then it's a good idea to put small windows on either side, as high as possible. On the inside of these windows you can secure a screen. Make sure that the perches are well under these opposing windows, so that you can open them during warm, muggy spells. It is important that you make sure you close these screens as soon as it begins to get too drafty or cold.

**Agapornis personatus,** *cobalt blue edged*

**Agapornis fischeri,** *sea green*

The usefulness of ionizers
If you have several birds, and you keep them in a limited space, such as a closed room or a shed, then purchasing an ionizer is definitely more than worth considering. Such apparati are not cheap but they have proven their usefulness. Ionizers make sure that miniscule particles of dust, such as pollen and flakes that hang around in the air, settle on the ground. The result is that neither the birds nor you can inhale the particles, or at least only in much smaller quantities, so the lungs are not so badly affected. Moreover, the atmosphere in a room where there is an ionizer working becomes fresher and cleaner. A good piece of apparatus can also reduce unpleasant smells.

# 4 CARE

## Hygiene

Hygiene is a key issue if you want to avoid health problems for your birds. If the aviary or cage is well–maintained, regularly disinfected, and the food and water trays are regularly washed, then bacteria will have no chance of making your birds sick. It is difficult to give any hard and fast rules about how often this needs to take place. It mainly depends on factors such as the size of the cage or aviary, the number of birds kept, the season, and the amount of dirtiness that builds up. In the summer, bacteria can and will spread more easily and quickly. For that reason alone, you will need to clean more often in the summer. It makes sense to clean the walls, the floor, the bars, and the perches regularly, with disinfectant. It is best to purchase these cleaning materials from a specialist pet shop, as not every disinfectant is safe for birds. It does often occur that people, thanks to cost cutting measures, simply decide to sieve the bottom covering.

*A hygienic environment prevents diseases and other problems*

Sieving gets rid of visible excrement and other messes, so that the bottom layer looks clean. But, in reality, the invisible germs, bacteria, and such like, are left behind. So it's better not to sieve the bottom covering. When you're cleaning the bottom covering of the cage or night compartment, it's best to get rid of it all, disinfect the bottom, and then add a fresh new layer. Invisible bacteria can also accumulate in water bottles that have a reservoir. Lovebirds do not drink very much, and the contents of the bottle often stay looking clean and clear. This is why some people only change the contents once or twice a week. In practice, it is essential to do this every day, so that bacteria aren't given a chance.

## Claws

If your lovebird has access to sufficient perches with different diameters, they do not usually grow claws that become

A taranta couple
*(fallow)*

too long. If this does happen, however, it is important to clip them. Claws that are too long are a hindrance to the animal, and they can also cause growths on the toes and feet. If you have to clip claws for the first time, it can be a gruesome job. Many people are scared to clip them "in real life," and this anxiety is not without reason. It can cause the claw to bleed–sometimes for a long time–and so the clipping can become a painful and traumatic experience for your bird. Therefore, you should only clip the very end of the claw. If you do not want to do it, ask an experienced bird breeder to do it for you.

**Agapornis personatus,** *sky blue*

**Agapornis roseicollis**

## Bath water

A daily bath or shower is essential to keep lovebirds healthy. You can shower your bird everyday by spraying it from a distance with water, using a plant sprayer. You can also choose to let it bathe itself. Using a pottery dish as a bath is the most practical. These can be cleaned hygienically and will not tip over if the bird stands on the edge. Let your birdbath always be there, and make sure that the water is changed daily, even if it doesn't look dirty. If you're giving your lovebird a shower, make sure that the water is not too cold. Cold and wet conditions can be disastrous for a lovebird, so avoid wetness in combination with a draft, even if it's high summer.

## Molting

Molting is a normal, annual changing of the feather coating. It usually occurs in the late summer or fall and lasts, under optimal circumstances, about a month. Because the molting process requires lots of energy, a good diet is of crucial importance. It is not an unnecessary luxury to provide some extra power food with specific vitamins. Power food, along with "molting vitamins," are on sale in small portions in pretty much every specialist pet shop. Make sure, especially during the molting season, that you give the bird a chance to wash everyday. If your animal doesn't take a bath of its own accord, give it a "shower" with a plant sprayer, from a reasonable distance. If you are looking after your bird properly, and the molting lasts longer than it should, it can be an indication of underlying problems. In that case, consult a bird veterinarian to make sure.

**Agapornis nigrigenis,** *lutino*

*Crusted dirt can easily be removed from the bottom pans of cages with scrapers like these*

**Agapornis nigrigenis,** *mauve*

# 5 Socialization, Behavior and Upbringing

## Socialization and upbringing, is it necessary?

Most people know that it is necessary for dogs to be well socialized and brought up. If the breeder or owner has split up a group of puppies, a dog will have an increased chance of behavioral problems, and all kinds of social difficulties in its later life. That lovebirds need to be socialized and brought up properly to avoid problems has not been known for very long. It is, however, very important that the socialization of lovebirds occurs, especially if they are going to be kept as pets. A lovebird that has grown up in a hut and has had only a little contact with people will have difficulty feeling happy in a family environment. This is certainly the case if the animal is already somewhat older. A bird of the same type that was born in a house, has been handled a lot, and has had positive experiences with people will, in contrast, become tame much quicker, and will not find household situations and happenings (vacuum cleaner, children, television) so stressful. The owner will also quickly notice the difference in

*A well brought up lovebird will not develop behavioral problems so often*

the way well socialized and badly socialized birds react to all kinds of new things, such as games. Socialization is therefore very important, but the same goes for their upbringing. A well brought up lovebird will not develop behavioral problems as often as an animal that has been badly brought up, or not brought up at all. Lovebirds have got a reputation for sometimes biting. They are also often accused of being excessively screechy. This kind of behavioral problem can often be traced to faults in their socialization, upbringing, and/or abusive treatment. To prevent problems, it is advisable to dip, somewhat, in to the psyche of a lovebird.

## Tame or not tame?

Most people that want a lovebird as a pet like it if the animal is, or can be made, tame. It has also become known that older animals that have trust in people can pass that trust on to their young. Older animals that have had bad experiences with people, or who haven't socialized well, teach their young that they have to be on their guard. If you want a tame lovebird, it is therefore preferable to choose an animal whose parents have trust in people. For socialization, it is best if the animals have grown up in a house. If you choose a young animal that has not been brought up in a house by untamed parents, then there is a good chance that the animal will have learnt that it has to be wary of people. This does not necessarily mean that the animal will

*If you want a tame bird, purchase an animal that has been used to people from a young age*

never become tame. Making such an animal tame does take more effort, though. It is essential that the animal is brought in to a house at a very young age (about 8 weeks), and that you have a lot of time for your new housemate. Very occasionally, hand–reared lovebirds are available. These animals are so used to–and focused on–people, that they are in fact already completely tame. They don't need any more taming.

*Making an older bird tame requires a lot of patience–this bird is obviously alert*

## Taming

If you don't have a bird that comes from a breeder, or one from untamed parents, then you will have to tame it your-self. The ground rule for this is that the animal must have trust in you, and learn that you will not do it any harm. Put the cage at eye level, so that you do not have to bend over the cage to speak with the bird–as this can often be a very frightening experience. Always treat your animal calmly, and speak in a friendly way when you give it food or drink, or when you want to give it a treat. Use the same words when doing this, such as "food," "snack," "water," and "shower," so that it will eventually understand what you mean. Lovebirds are extremely intelligent birds. Tasty treats can also be very helpful in the taming process. You can offer your bird something that it will find tasty, such as a small piece of millet or chickweed, several times a day,

*It has become apparent that young animals from tame parents are easier to tame than the young from animals that are anxious around people*

through the bars at first. If it goes from one side of the cage to the other in a state of panic, or looks at you suspiciously, stay calm and persevere. Always talk to it in a calm, friendly tone. It can take longer with one bird than with another, but eventually almost all lovebirds will become too curious to stay anxious. When your bird eats out of your hand then you have won the first bit of trust. You can consequently build the contact up slowly, until it is no longer scared when you offer it something through the bars, and it comes to eat your offering without reservation. Only then can you open the door to offer it something tasty from inside its cage. Never make unexpected movements and, most of all, be patient, and don't try to grab it. Also, do not pull your hand away if you think it's going to bite. This can make it very scared and put you back a step. In order to create calm, it is best to practice when you're alone, so that neither you nor the bird can be distracted. You will notice yourself when the bird is beginning to trust you. You can then gently and occasionally try to tickle its breast. When it eventually finds it okay for you to gently stroke or tickle it, then you can try to use your finger as a "step" by holding your finger against its breast. Only when your lovebird steps on to your finger or hand without hesitation, is it ready to be let out of its cage for the first time.

## Teaching your bird to step onto your hand

Lovebirds are very investigative, curious, and intelligent, and they love to be able to spread their wings. Once a bird is tame, you can let it fly freely in the living room for several hours a day without worry, on the condition that you always keep an eye on it. It is not recommended that you simply let your bird loose. It's better to first teach your animal to step onto an outstretched finger or hand, and so bring it out of the cage. From an upbringing perspective, this is better than letting the bird go in and out of the cage on its own. It is apparent that birds that are able to choose for themselves if and when they want to leave the cage, sometimes develop territorial aggression. That means that they can react aggressively if someone puts a hand in their cage (their territory). By teaching a bird to step onto a finger or hand that will take it out of the cage, it learns two important things. First of all it learns to associate a finger or hand being put in its cage with something nice, namely playtime. Secondly, in this manner, it learns that this is the only way for it to get out of its cage. Bad behavior can so be avoided, to a point. If a tame bird does attack your finger, close the door and don't let it out of its cage. Your lovebird will eventually understand from this that aggressive behavior, such as biting, does

*Lovebirds often use their beak to help get a grip before "stepping"–Do not pull your hand away too quickly if you think your animal is going to bite*

*Lovebirds who can go in and out of their cage of their own accord often develop territorial aggression*

not bring any advantages. It does, in fact, bring just the opposite, but "well–behaved stepping" does work. Do not make the mistake of thinking that it is trying to bite you when it tries to grab your finger with its beak. Lovebirds often use their beak to get a grip before they "step up." So do not pull your hand away too quickly. It makes sense to associate a word with this action of stepping. In this case it doesn't matter what word you use, as long as it is always the same, so that the bird can make the association between hearing the word and stepping on your finger. As soon as your lovebird knows what the word means, and follows your "command," you can also use it for other situations.

## Loose in the house

Before you let your bird fly freely in your house or living room, make sure that the room is actually safe to let it do so. For this, check the following things:
• Are there any poisonous plants? (see also "Illnesses" chapter)
• Are the curtains closed, so that your lovebird can't accidentally fly into the glass?
• Are all (electrical) wires well–hidden behind strong skirting boards?
• Are there any animals present that the bird could chase?
• Are all the doors closed?
• Is there an open fire (gas furnace, open hearth) or a hot boiler that could wound your animal?
• Have you covered any aquariums or fish bowls so that your bird cannot fall in (and drown)?

## Getting it back in the cage

Most lovebirds will go back into their cage themselves when they have had enough of being loose in the room. They will either be hungry, thirsty, or will simply want to go back in their cage. If you want to get your lovebird back in its cage somewhat quicker, then you can try and tempt it back in with tasty treats. It will also help if you can get it to step on your finger, and so put it back in its cage. If none of this works, and it's important that you get your bird back in its cage, then there is no choice but to capture it. Try and keep this sort of action to a minimum, as it can be very stressful for your animal. If you do need to capture your bird, first darken the room and then capture it by throwing a tea towel over it. If darkening the room is quickly followed by the catching of the bird, then its eyes will not have had enough time to get used to the dark. If you also refrain from speaking to the bird, and you put it straight into its home, then the capture is not, or is at least much less, associated with you.

## Preventing biting

Nearly all lovebirds like to nibble on something with their beaks. As long as it happens on toys there is nothing to worry about, and nobody will find this behavior irritating. However, if your bird does nibble you, or somebody else, this can turn into very painful biting. This type of biting behavior doesn't just start on its own. It always begins with gentle nibbling that is not experienced as biting by owners,

*Biting behavior can be prevented through correct upbringing*

though it eventually becomes real biting. In order to prevent your bird from developing this biting behavior, it is advisable to teach it, from a young age, that nibbling (read biting!) people is not allowed. You do this by consistently always setting your lovebird down somewhere if it nibbles or bites you. You can also say "no!" admonishingly. Do offer it an alternative option straightaway, by giving it a toy or a piece of paper that it can ruin. If you keep this up consistently, then in the future it will often be sufficient to just say "no!" to it. Then your bird knows that he's not allowed to do it.

## Hormonal aggression towards people

Aggressive biting behavior towards people happens a lot. The aggression is often directed at a certain person in the family, but sometimes the bird can react aggressively to everyone in the family. The (continuation of) biting can occur for different reasons. The two most common reasons are mistakes in upbringing, and hormones in female birds. Hormonal aggression only occurs in female lovebirds. The aggression can be directed at the person in the house with whom the bird has the strongest bond, but also at everybody else, who it might see as "intruders" whom must be chased away from her nest. Sometimes the animal lays eggs, or collects nesting material, during aggressive periods. In such cases, the cause is obvious. Hormonal aggression really is a big problem because it keeps coming back. The animal will not bite as long as it doesn't have any desire to breed, but it can get into a rage, all of a sudden, when the days get longer. If you have a lovebird that displays this behavior from time to time then you can choose to keep her shut in her cage for these periods. Give her enough food and distraction, but don't let her out of her home as long as her aggressive period continues. If you have tried everything, and she stays aggressive, it is sometimes better to give her a male partner. Sometimes this can mean that giving her to somebody else, who would like to use her for breeding, is the only remaining option. Mistakes in upbringing are another cause of biting behavior. Lovebirds benefit from a strict hierarchy in the house, and it is important that your bird understands that you are higher up in the ranking than it is. If you have taught your bird to step onto your hand, and have always been consistent, then there is less of a chance that your bird will become aggressive. If you do let the bird leave its cage of its own accord, and think that is fine, there is a good chance that it will see this as a weakness on your part, and so it

**Agapornis roseicollis**

increases the chance that it will bite you. It will not help to then go and scream or become angry at your bird – this will have an adverse effect. It is important for your bird to learn that there are boundaries, and that it is you, and not it, who determines where these boundaries lie. It is also important that you stick to these boundaries consistently.

## Laying an egg

Some female lovebirds do sometimes lay eggs, even if they are kept on their own. It has been said, of this phenomenon, that it means the bird feels extremely comfortable with herself.

> Punishment for the bird that should not be allowed:
> Lovebirds can be punished by saying "no!" to them angrily, and by putting the animal in a separate cage that is not its own. What you really must never do is hit the bird, scream at it, or tap its beak. That will not get rid of the unwanted behavior, and can lead to the animal becoming even more aggressive—often because it has simply become scared.

Even though I do not want to dispute this, the laying of an egg is more likely to be a hormonal occurrence that is activated by (a change in) diet, or the offering of nesting material (a "little hut" or breeding place). It is often just a single egg,

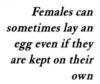

*Females can sometimes lay an egg even if they are kept on their own*

but it can also be the case that your bird will lay an egg every day for up to nine days. This depends on the condition of your lovebird. Because the eggs are from a single pet kept on its own, they cannot be fertilized, and so it is better not to encourage the laying of eggs. It is best to just let the laid eggs stay where they are, because regularly removing the eggs will stimulate a new egg to be laid. If you let the eggs stay where they are laid, it is very possible that your pet will, at a given time, attempt to incubate it – certainly if the bird has a nesting place at its disposal. After three weeks it will become apparent to the bird that the egg is not going to produce any young, and she will lose interest. Only then is it recommended that you take the egg away. If you give her extra egg feed and calcium during the period that she is laying and incubating eggs, her condition will not suffer too much.

*The shrill and piercing voice can be very disturbing for many people*

### Preventing too much noise

Lovebirds are well known for their shrill and piercing voices. The squawking is a completely normal characteristic of lovebirds. In the wild, they mainly squawk to keep in contact with each other over long distances. If a lovebird spends a lot of its day squawking, it can be perceived as a problematic experience. Not only by the owners, but also by those living nearby. It helps to throw a cover over the cage. This will create an artificial night when the bird is always quiet. It is a very common method for reducing loud, squawking behavior. But excessive squawking often has a cause. It makes sense to determine what this cause is so that efforts can be made to remove it. It is even better to prevent your bird from squawking excessively, by not giving it a reason to do so. The most common causes of excessive squawking behavior are as follows:

#### • Boredom

A lovebird that is bored will look for all kinds of distractions to occupy it. Lots of them come to the conclusion that squawking can be a pleasant pastime. If you make sure that the animal has enough to do in and out of its home, then there is much less of a chance that it will squawk so much.

## • Attention

Lovebirds are very sociable birds. If your bird is not getting enough attention, then it can squawk out of boredom. If it notices that this brings it attention, it can make a habit out of it. It doesn't matter to your lovebird if it is getting positive or negative attention. So getting angry makes no sense at all. As far the bird is concerned, all attention, even negative attention, is attention nonetheless. And so its squawking behavior is rewarded. It is, therefore, best to always ignore your lovebird when it is squawking for attention. If you think that your lovebird has developed this squawking behavior as a result of receiving too little attention, build some method in to your day to give it attention. But do not choose the moments that it is squawking to do this, as this will only strengthen its belief in its unwanted behavior.

## • Intermittent care

Lovebirds are, and this cannot be stressed enough, very intelligent birds. As soon as their food or water tray is empty, or if they want a piece apple or something else, they will start squawking to let this be known. If you respond to the "demands" of the bird, there will be an increased chance of your animal continuing to squawk every time it wants something that you can give it, until you understand and give it what it wants. It speaks for itself that you can prevent this from happening by making sure you always give it

*Right:*
**Agapornis
nigrigenis,**
*light green
multicolored*

*Left:*
**Agapornis lilianae**

*Lovebirds can learn a lot, more than most people think*

enough food and water. Furthermore, it is important never to react to squawking behavior, as this will only condition its behavior further. If you do forget to give it enough food, and this is brought to your attention by its squawking, then it's important to wait until it stops squawking before you feed it. This prevents the bird from being rewarded for squawking.

## If nothing helps

It can happen that birds keep on squawking even if they are getting enough attention, have lots of good care, and have enough to do. The squawking can simply have become a habit or a way of demanding your attention at times when you aren't, or can't be, giving it attention. With some effort on your part, you can train your bird to be quiet very well, or at least to squawk more quietly, by giving it a "command." You do this by being very consistent. If your bird starts squawking at a time that it really shouldn't, you can use a certain word or short sentence that you would never use otherwise. For example, "You have to be quiet now!" Then cover half of its home with a sheet. If your bird keeps on squawking, say the word or sentence that you use exclusively again, and pull the cover further over the cage. If the bird still carries on, then cover the cage completely and wait at least a quarter of an hour before removing the cover again. Take note—the bird must have quieted down before you remove the cover, otherwise this process does not serve any purpose. So be consistent—you warn it twice, and then the third time, you "punish" it by completely covering the cage with a sheet. There are very few lovebirds that enjoy having to sit in a darkened cage on a bright day. This, coupled with the high intelligence of the animals, means that there is a very good chance your bird will quickly get the message that it has to be quiet whenever you tell it "You have to be quiet now!" In spite of all this, it is important that you honestly ask yourself if your animal really is being offered enough attention, care and entertainment, before employing this method. Furthermore, it is also important to give the bird the chance to have a good squawk every now and then. It is, after all, natural behavior for a lovebird. You cannot completely stop your animal from behaving in this way, and it is not desirable or fair to the animal in any case.

**Agapornis personatus,** *lutino*

**Agapornis nigrigenis,** *Sky blue*

# 6 ACTIVITY THERAPY

*p. 73:*
Olive green
taranta

## Activity therapy

A lovebird is a bird that is naturally very investigative and curious, and it also needs something to be busy with. In a stale (read boring) home, there is a good chance that the animal will show certain stereotypical behavioral traits, or just sit and stare apathetically. Also, squawking, biting, and other traits often have their origin in boredom. That's why it's good to make sure that the bird has enough things to do. There are various kinds of toys available to buy, ranging from willow twigs to leather toys (that it can gnaw to pieces), to little swings, bells, steps, and seesaws. You can also make your bird some toys. Always remember that one bird is not necessarily like another. Just because one bird enjoys a toy, does not mean that another bird will enjoy it too. It might not be interested at all. It is therefore preferable to give it as many different toys as possible, so that you can find out what your bird likes doing best. Because lovebirds are so intelligent, they usually get bored of a toy after a couple of weeks. That's why it's a good idea to regularly

*Lovebirds often get bored of a toy after a few weeks*

change the toys for new, totally different ones. This will mean your bird always has something new to play with, and so it stays exciting for it. You can also choose to hide certain toys for a while, and only bring them out again every so often.

## Gnawing

There are different toys for sale, or that can be made, on which your bird gnaw. Small pieces of paper, sisal ropes, and twigs from willow trees or fruit trees, are all very good for this purpose. You can, for example, hang a long sisal rope in the bird's home, from the top of the cage to the bottom, so that the bird can climb onto it at the bottom and climb all the way to the top. But you can also make a sort of swing out of it, or hang it in various crisscrossing ways, in the cage. Lots of lovebirds like to shred paper to pieces. You can use the inside of a toilet roll, or other bits

*Willow stick*

of paper for this, and simply put them, or hang them up in the cage.

*A rosiecollis couple in a special "lovebird tent"*

## Hiding
Hiding things is also a game that the average lovebird will enjoy. You can get specially made "sleeping bags" and "tents" for this, but a strong paper bag can also be used for hiding things, or simply for playing with.

## Mirrors, reflectors
While you are looking through the many toys that are available for sale for lovebirds, you will also come across mirrors. These toys are somewhat controversial. Even though a lovebird is generally seen as a clever bird, it probably doesn't understand that it is being confronted with its own mirror image. This is noticeable from the sometimes very strong "bond" that they maintain with their mirror. People therefore presume that the bird thinks it is playing with its playmate. Some birds become so fixated with their mirror

*Bells come in all shapes, sizes and models—make sure they are strong enough!*

that they don't even look at their owner. That's why it's better not to purchase a mirror. It can make the bird a little crazy, and can sometimes lead to your bird being much less responsive towards you.

### Scared of toys?
Most lovebirds are mad about all kinds of toys, and they can't be changed often enough. New toys are investigated and tested with lots of enthusiasm. But it can also happen

*Sisal rope*

that the bird seems to be scared of a toy. And some birds always react anxiously if something new is put, or hung, in their home. This does not need to be a reason for not giving the bird any toys at all, because an anxious bird can quickly become despondent. In such a case it is better to let the bird get used to the new toy gradually. You do this by putting or hanging the toy a few tens of centimeters away from the cage at first, so that the bird can see it from a safe place. As long as the bird keeps reacting well (and so not anxiously), the toy can be brought a little closer to the

*Colorful leather toys*

*Nearly all lovebirds think swings are really good toys*

cage every day, until you can hang it on the outside of the cage. If the bird has become curious, you can hang it up in the cage. This way of introducing toys usually goes without a hitch. Do not forget that another new toy must, once again, be introduced in the same way.

## Safety for all

Nearly all toys, even if they have been specially made for lovebirds, can be broken. And they will break if your bird plays with them too enthusiastically. This is often not a problem, but it is always a good idea to check the toys well. Are there any bits that could be swallowed? Points or sharp parts? Could, for example, a tear in material cause your bird to get its feet or beak caught? It speaks for itself that any toys that are broken, or that could eventually be a danger to the bird, should be thrown away.

**Agapornis fischeri,** *light green pastel*

*p. 81:*
*A cross between*
*an* A. fischeri *and*
*an* A. personatus

# 7 Diet

## Tasty isn't automatically good

Various studies have been done on the natural living and eating habits of the most common types of lovebirds, such as the Rosiecollis, in the wild. The animals live off whatever is available during the season in question, and what best meets their dietary needs. As soon as another season begins, and there are new plant and grass seeds available, or if there are new bunches of berries, the animals will take what they can. It has become apparent that most lovebirds eat grass seeds, but they also sometimes eat rice, berries, green food, and fruit. Very occasionally, namely in the breeding season, they will also eat animal protein, such as insects. But lovebirds that we keep as pets don't have this abundant choice of different food types. They have to make do with what we can offer them, and this often means that they get too much

*Tasty doesn't
necessarily mean
healthy*

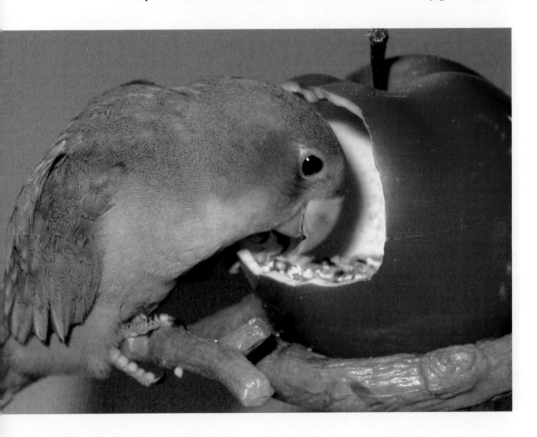

fatty and protein rich foods given to them. In practice, it also seems that many birds that are kept as pets cannot make a distinction between food that is, and food that is not (any longer), suitable for them to eat. Boredom can be the cause of the eating of unsuitable, bad (off), or even poisonous foods. Avocados, for example, are very poisonous to some lovebirds. Most birds will eat this, though, if they find it in their cage or aviary, even with all the disastrous consequences it brings. It's also true that lovebirds have a strong preference for fatty and protein rich foods. Sunflower seeds, egg feed, and even cake and tarts are enjoyed, at the expense of eating much healthier food that is lower in calories. This, together with the fact that most pet lovebirds get much less exercise than birds of the same type in the wild, means that many animals become obese. Moreover, food that is too high in fat, protein, or carbohydrate (sugar) can cause digestive problems. It can also, in the long term, lead to chronic health problems. That's why it's so important for a lovebird owner to give their animals a good quality, well–balanced diet, and to make sure they get enough exercise.

A lovebird's menu
• Lovebird's seed mixture or ready made pellets
• Fruit, vegetables and green foods
• Stomach gravel
• Millet
• Fresh (not too cold) water

*Mixed seeds*

## How much food?

It is not easy to work out how many grams of food a love-bird needs per day because it very much depends on the situation and circumstances. Does the animal live inside or outside? Is it busy with nesting and breeding? Is it the molting season? What is the temperature of its environment, and how much does the bird actually move? All these types of things have an influence on their dietary requirements. On average, a lovebird gets enough nourishment from two soupspoons of mixed seed per day, topped off with fruit and vegetables. In practice, it is very rare that birds do not get enough to eat. It is much more often the case, especially with tame caged birds, that it's the other way round, and they get too much to eat. Aside from the fact that eating too much is unhealthy, an abundance of food can make a bird very choosy. If there are too many foodstuffs available, a lovebird will quickly pick all the tastiest bits out of the food, and just let the rest lie there. The tastiest bits are often rich in fat, like peanuts and sun-flower seeds. If you want to keep your bird healthy, it is recommended to always give it only small amounts of food. This will keep it looking forward to its food, and it will eat most of the seeds, even those that are not so tasty, but are healthy.

## Pellets – the new ready made food

A few years ago a new type of food was taken to Europe from the United States–pellets. Pellets are small blocks of food that contain all the foodstuffs that your bird needs.

*Pellets*

Feeding your bird pellets has its advantages and disadvantages. A big advantage is that a lovebird cannot fish the tastiest seeds out of its food, and leave the rest.

Pellets all have the same constitution. They also produce much less of a mess, because the birds do not need to shell or peel them. People who have a lot of birds, usually view the increased cost of this food, when compared to the classic seed mixtures, as a disadvantage. Two other arguments against this type of food are not based on fact, but are rumors based mainly on emotional grounds. Those who are against this type of food argue that it is too far removed from the bird's natural diet in the wild. It is also argued that the food is not exciting enough for a bird, because the constitution of each pellet is the same, and therefore also tastes the same—but this is possibly just a (too) human idea. It is a fact that pellets have been used in the United States for years, and they have produced very good results.

Constipation:
Constipation, a known problem in caged birds, is often not directly linked to their diet, but is more often a consequence of too little exercise.

## What do I need to look out for?

Aside from the fact that in nature, seeds serve as food for all sorts of animals, the primary purpose of seeds is, of course, to germinate and grow into new plants or trees. So seeds are also living things. Under certain circumstances, they can be liable to decay. To prevent this from happening, the seeds need to be stored in optimal conditions, not only by the importer or wholesaler and shop, but also by the consumer at home. It is best to keep your lovebird's seed mixture well closed away in a cool, dry, and preferably dark room. It is better to buy small containers than large ones, even if the small ones are more expensive. Food deteriorates in quality and, after a period of time, the vitamin content can be substantially reduced. Have a good look to see if the quality of the seeds is good. For example, it should not be dusty or smell musty, but should shine.

## Fruit, vegetables, berries and green food

Lovebirds are seed-eaters. A well-balanced lovebird's menu is not made up only of seeds, but also of softer foods such as fruits and vegetables. These last ingredients are bursting with vitamins and other important foodstuffs. They therefore also belong on every lovebird's menu. If you are giving your bird fruits and vegetables, try to vary them as much as possible. It is better to give a little bit of everything, than to just give apples or pears every day. You can collect green food, such as herbs, from the wild, but this can have some disadvantages. The herbs and fruit can be polluted by fallout from heavy industry, exhaust fumes, and pesticides. Never give food that is wilted, rotten or even moldy. Take away food that is not being eaten on time. Egg feed is a supplementary food that contains animal protein. Egg feed is, therefore, also a necessary foodstuff for animals who need to get stronger, or are very young and still growing. It is also essential before, during, and after the nesting period. Because it contains a lot of calories, it is better to only give mouthfuls, or none at all, during other phases of life.

Examples of suitable fruits and vegetables

- Apricots (dried or fresh)
- Pineapples
- Sweet apples
- Bananas
- Dates
- Grapes
- Corncobs
- Mandarins
- Pawpaw (papaya)
- Pears
- Fresh raisins and currants
- Celery (in small amounts)
- Grapefruit segments
- Tomatoes
- Figs
- Carrots

Examples of suitable berries

- Blackberries
- Raspberries
- Rowan berries
- Hawthorn berries
- Rose hips
- Pyracantha
- Elderberries

## Stomach gravel

Seed eating birds such as lovebirds have evolved their digestive systems to be able to digest this food. Lovebirds have stomach muscles that make the seed very fine, so that it can be digested more easily. This process can only work if the stomach muscle also contains some bird sand or sharp stomach gravel, that works as a sort of millstone. The bird itself digests the gravel and the sand, as necessary. It doesn't stay present in the stomach muscle forever. When the sharp edges are worn, the gravel and the sand are transported further and excreted. If the seed–eating bird cannot digest any sand or gravel then it is more difficult for it to digest its

Examples of suitable green plants:

- Fresh seeds of grasses
- Shepherd's purse
- Tansy ragwort *(Senecio jacobaea)*
- Yarrow
- Coltsfoot
- Sow thistle
- Dandelion
- Peach (seeds and blossoms)
- Evening primrose *(Oenothera biennis)*
- Garden cress
- Chickweed *(Stellaria media)*
- Ribwort plantain

harder foods. In a specialist pet shop, you can buy sharp stomach gravel for parakeets and lovebirds that often also contains charcoal. Give the bird a small tray of such a mixture once a week, so that it can digest what it needs.

*Stomach gravel*

*Grit*

## Calcium, vitamins and minerals

If you offer your lovebird a varied menu, with pellets as the main ingredient, or mixed seeds for lovebirds, it should not be a problem. There are, however, phases of life when a bird needs extra foodstuffs. During laying, for example, some extra calcium is badly needed–the bird must somehow make the eggshells from it. Growing birds, whose skeleton is getting bigger, also need extra calcium. You can hang a squid's skeleton, better known by the name of "sepia" or "cuttlefish," in the cage, so that the animals can take as much as they need.

*There are all kinds of types and shapes of snacks*

## Snacks

Snacks for lovebirds come in all shapes, sizes, smells, colors, and tastes. Everyone who has one or more lovebirds as a pet will be tempted, at least once every now and then, to pick up such a brightly colored "snack bell" or chew stick from the pet shop or supermarket. And there is nothing wrong with that, as long as you realize that too much is not good for it. So only give such snacks in moderation, even if they have been specially made for birds. Fresh willow twigs to nibble on, and small pieces of fruit and green food, are at least as nice for the birds, but moreover they contain much fewer calories.

**Agapornis fischeri**

p. 91:
*This* A.
personatus *is an
exception—one
side is blue and
the other side is
green*

# 8 BREEDING

## The beginning

The scope of this book does not reach far enough to cover all the ins and outs of how the breeding of lovebirds should be handled. There are several diverse and outstanding books available for people who only purchase lovebirds with the intention of breeding them. This chapter is, therefore, written for the hobbyist who only has one pair or a few pairs of lovebirds, and thinks it would be good to let them breed.

## Gender distinctions

The genders of lovebirds are not visible from their exteriors, with the exception of the Agapornis canus, A. pullarius, and A. taranta. There are different methods for determining the correct gender of the birds.

*The gender of the* fischeri *cannot be seen from its exterior*

### • The shape of the tail
The shape of the tail can give a good indication as to a bird's gender, but this method is unfortunately not watertight. The females usually have a squarer end to their tail, whereas those of males are more pointed.

### • The "beak test"
The so-called beak test is the most effective method for experienced breeders. Somebody who has experience at this can determine whether it is a male or a female, by feeling the beak bones and taking into account the distance between them. This method, however, seems to be everything but watertight, considering that even the most experienced people can still make mistakes. Furthermore, this method

**Fischeri,**
*Dark green*

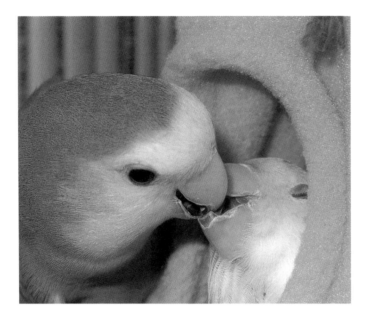

*The feeding of another bird is a behavioral trait that males have*

can only be carried out when the animal is at least 8 or 9 months old.

### • DNA test
There are different methods for determining the gender of birds using DNA tests. One of these methods is by taking a blood sample. It is best to get a specialist bird veterinarian to take this blood sample. The veterinarians can sometimes test the sample themselves, or it can be sent to a laboratory. There are also a few laboratories where bird owners can get their bird's gender determined without the intervention of a veterinarian. These laboratories don't process blood samples. It is sufficient for the bird owner to simply send some of the bird's breast feathers.

### • Behavior
The behavior of the bird can give a good indication as to the bird's gender in many cases. Birds can often show certain behavioral patterns once they are sexually mature. Males can follow their chosen ones, and can also display "riding behavior" on objects, or even people. As soon as a bird lays an egg it is, of course, obvious that it's a female. Making a nest is also typical behavior for female lovebirds, and so gives an obvious indication. When a group of lovebirds are kept together, couples often split themselves off from the group during mating season. If you have the possibility of

waiting for this season, then you can simply separate the formed couples from the other birds.

• **Endoscopic inspection**
Sexually mature birds can undergo an endoscopic inspection at a specialist bird veterinarian's practice. This involves making a very small incision in the bird's stomach, so that the veterinarian can look at the internal reproductive organs with an endoscope. The bird is always anaesthetized for this. In practice, this method is almost never used on lovebirds. Consultation with a specialist bird veterinarian is necessary, and most lovebird hobbyists find the cost of this too high. That's why this method is more commonly used on parrots, who are much more expensive to purchase, and for whom the gender can be decisive when determining the price, and whether to go through with the sale or not.

## When to breed?
Your lovebirds cannot breed on demand. They have to be in the right mood. Factors such as a richer diet, and the pres-

---

In short:
- Lovebirds become sexually mature at approximately 9 months
- It is better not to use animals for breeding until they are 11-13 months old
- The average size of a nest is 3 to 7 eggs
- The incubation period lasts about 21 days
- When the young are about 8 weeks old, they can get by without their parents

---

ence of nesting huts and materials, can get the birds in the right mood. So it does not depend on the number of daylight hours, as is the case with many other birds. In the regions that lovebirds originally come from, the number of daylight hours is pretty much the same in the winter as it is in the summer. If the animals get a richer, more varied diet in winter, they can also start breeding then. It speaks for itself that this is not an ideal situation, as it is often too cold for their young. Furthermore, in the winter, the nights are too long. Lovebirds only eat if it is light. In the evenings they sleep. If there are too few daylight hours, and the nights are very long and cold, it can have fatal consequences

for young animals. So it's best to let your lovebirds breed in the spring or summer months, as long as the climate conditions are favorable.

*Richer foods are necessary during the breeding season*

## Diet during the breeding season

The building of a nest, the laying and incubating of eggs, and caring for the young, demands a lot of energy from the birds. It is therefore logical that the diet deserves extra attention during the breeding season. But the animals' diet must contain more calories even before they begin to nest, so that they can be in the best possible condition before starting on this demanding task. If you give them more protein rich food in January, they will be ready for breeding in March. If you feed your lovebirds a seed mixture, then it's best to also start giving them some egg feed, along with their seed mixture, from January. If you give ready-made pellets, then gradually switch over to pellet foods that are specially made for the breeding season. Keep giving the egg

feed or special pellets until about a month after the last of the young have flown away. After that, normal feeding can safely be resumed.

## Nesting boxes

In the wild, different types of lovebird each have their own type-specific preference for certain nesting places. For most kept and bred types, such as the Fischeri, the Personatus and the Rosiecollis, standard lovebirds' nesting boxes, that can be purchased in specialist pet shops, are appropriate. These wooden nesting boxes typically have measurements of about 10 inches across, 8 inches deep and 6 inches high. It is better for them to be wider than they are high. The diameter of the entrance hole should be about 2 or 3 inches. Attach the nesting box securely to the cage or aviary, so that no accidents can happen.

## Aggression

Some hobbyists prefer to give their animals as natural environment as possible, and just leave them alone to do what they do naturally. If you are keeping several couples of love-

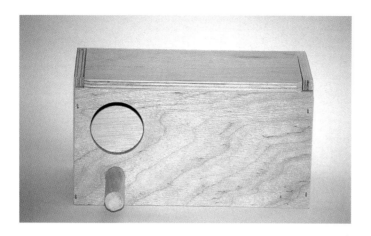

*Nesting box*

birds together in an aviary, take into account that most types can sometimes, during the mating season, become very aggressive towards each other, and towards other birds. These types are, therefore, best kept as separate couples. Only the Nigrigenis and Lilianae often breed without a problem when in a group. In this case, take into account the fact that problems can arise, for example, over favorite nesting places. To prevent this from happening, you can hang all the nesting boxes at the same height, at a reasonable distance from each other. This will ensure that no argument can ensue about the nesting boxes in the highest places, that are often thought of as being the best. It also makes sense to hang not just one, but two nesting boxes next to each other, for each couple. This brings peace to the colony, and the chance is small that they will try and take over each others' nesting boxes.

*Three young*
**A. rosiecollis**
*from one nest*

## Nest material and building a nest

Your lovebirds need nesting material in order to dress their nests. You can make diverse thin willow twigs available to them, along with millet stems, hay, coconut fibers, and even wood chippings. The chippings can be laid on the bottom of the nesting boxes, so that the birds can work with them further. It is best to hang millet stems and willow twigs at a reasonable height in the cage or aviary—on the ground they can become dirty. All in all, the building of a nest takes an average of two weeks. During this time, the female keeps herself busy building the nest. The male looks after her, by feeding her, amongst other things.

## The eggs and incubation period

The first egg is usually laid at least a week after the first successful pairing. From then on the female will usually lay a new egg every two days, until the total number is reached. This amount can vary widely, but is about 5 on average. The female sometimes begins to incubate the first egg as soon as it is laid, but most only begin with the second one. There are also some birds that wait until all of them have been laid. The incubation period lasts, on average, about 21 or 22 days, starting from the moment that the female actually begins incubation. If the female starts incubating as soon as the first egg is laid, then it is not unusual for all the eggs to

*Eggs never hatch all at the same time*

*Notice the big difference between the two young ones that have just hatched–this is normal*

hatch at different times. Some will only appear a few days later. You will then see differences in size and development, which in itself is not a problem. The male doesn't get involved with the incubation, but rather guards the nest and brings his partner food.

## Problems with hatching
It often happens that one or more eggs do not hatch. It is recommended, once the eggs have been incubated for about

*A very big nest of eggs–if the eggs do not hatch, there is a good chance that the couple is made up of two females*

10 days, to look and see, with a flashlight, if the eggs really have been fertilized. Developing—and therefore fertilized—eggs are then recognizable from the blood vessels that branch out from the shell. It is best to remove non-fertilized eggs. If your lovebird couple continuously produces non-fertilized eggs, it could well be because they are both female. If the eggs are fertilized and well incubated, but young ones fail to appear, the fault can usually be traced to too low a humidity in the nesting box. In this case give the animals more fresh willow twigs for the next round of breeding. These contain more moisture than the dried wood chippings or dry millet stems, and so the humidity in the nest is kept at a better level. It is also a good idea to put a bathing dish with fresh water in their box every day. During warm spells, the female will definitely be happy to make use of it, and so when she goes back onto her nest she will automatically moisten her eggs. On very warm days it can help to use a plant sprayer or sponge to dampen the outside of the nesting box. Ideal humidity is about 65%. Even though the low humidity is usually the problem, non-hatching eggs can also be the result of the temperature

*The dark patch on this lovebird is caused by a (temporary) carotene (vitamin A) deficiency, and is not hereditary*

*Make sure that
your birds are
used to you
checking the nest
regularly*

being too low. The ideal temperature is about 68 degrees
Fahrenheit (20 degrees Celsius).

## Rings

It is best to fix permanent foot rings to young birds. A fixed
foot ring mustn't be confused with a colored clip ring, that
can be attached to the feet of adult birds. Clip rings are used
to make a distinction between birds that otherwise look
very much alike. Fixed foot rings are unique to each bird
that has one, and they are permanent. A fixed foot ring can

---

Checking the nest
When your birds begin to hatch, you can start getting them used to you by
going and having a little look in their nesting box once or twice a day.
Once they are used to you, they will no longer protest if it is necessary to
check on them every now and then.

---

only be put on the legs of young nesting birds when they are
about 8 or 9 days old. After that, it is no longer possible to
get it on the animal, without causing it a lot of pain. If the

young ones are growing fast, it makes sense to put their rings on even earlier–this will avoid any surprises. Foot rings can be ordered from bird associations of which you are a member. If you are not a member of a bird association, then you can't ring your birds. That has the disadvantage that birds that you have bred can be seen as "illegally import-ed," especially if the bird is of a rare type. This can lead to problems for you, or for the people that you give your young birds to. Nobody can prove that these unringed birds were not born in the wild. It is therefore a good idea to become a member of a bird association and order a set of rings on time–even if it is only for a single occurrence of nesting. In some countries it is in fact obligatory to ring birds, and keep all the relevant administration in case it is ever needed.

*The rings work like this ...*

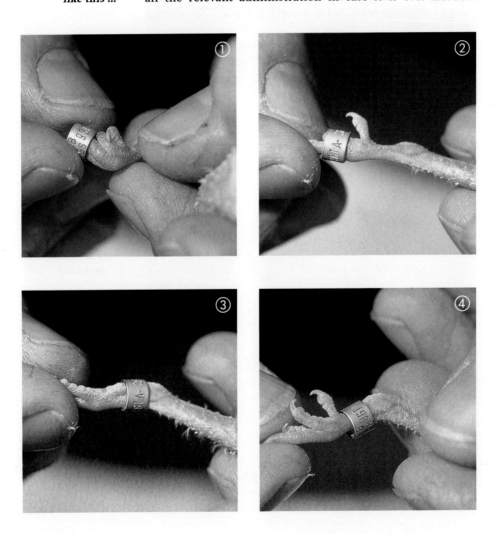

Everything can then be explained easily. Lovebirds use a ring with a diameter of approximately 0.18 inches. It can happen that the parents of the animal will try and remove the ring, probably because they think that these "shiny things" do not belong in the nest. It can help, in such a case, to color the rings black with a permanent waterproof marker pen. Then they are not so noticeable. The black layer will eventually wear away, with the process of time.

## Growing up

After the young have hatched, the female takes on the responsibility of feeding them. Make sure that you provide extra egg feed during this period, because it is just then that the young birds need more animal protein. The female keeps on feeding her young until they are about five or six weeks old. After that the male takes over this task. When the young are about eight weeks old, they are developed

Fixed ring sizes
0.16 inches Cana, Lilianae en Nigrigenis
0.18 inches Roseicollis, Taranta
0.17–0.18 inches Personata, Fischeri

*The female feeds her young until they are about 5 or 6 weeks old*

**Agapornis
nigrigenis,
*olive green***

enough to manage without their parents. By this time the female can already be busy with her next round of hatchlings.

## Aggression towards their own young

It often happens that the young from the first nest cannot yet stand on their own feet by the time the parents are busy with their next batch. Sometimes the parents can then react aggressively, and with hostility, towards their half grown up young. This can lead to dramas. If the animals are still too young to take care of themselves, you could decide to bring them up by hand. It happens quite a lot that lovebirds will pluck at feathers. Parents can sometimes pluck their young completely bald, and in extreme cases until they bleed. This (disturbed) behavior can occur for all kinds of reasons, and there is not a single, all encompassing solution. The reason could be boredom, too little (sun) light, or a change in diet, but there are always more and more reasons being suggested. It is possible, for instance, that it could be hereditary bad manners that can occur in certain family lines or branches. If the parents do indeed have too little to do, you can give them something to play with in the form of willow twigs. Sometimes the parents will stop the plucking if the lid of the nesting box is removed, or shifted slightly to one side, so that light comes into the box. There are also products available in the shops that you can apply to the young, but this only works temporarily. If nothing works, there is little choice but to remove the parent that is guilty of this behavior, and leave the remaining parent to take care of the young. If both parents are guilty of plucking feathers, then you would have to bring up the young by hand yourself. Many breeders, however, choose another method that often works very well. The young are put in a smaller cage that is, in turn, placed inside the bigger parent's home. There is a very good chance that the parents will instinctively keep on feeding their young through the bars, but in this way, the little ones are protected from their feather plucking parents. This is often a successful way of stopping the parents from threatening their young. Unfortunately, it does sometimes happen that female lovebirds pluck their young to death in the nest. This mostly happens if the mother is too young. A female lovebird should be at least 11 months old, and preferably even older, before she is used for breeding.

**Agapornis personatus,** *cobalt blue*

## Bringing the young up by hand

There are different situations conceivable that make it necessary for you to bring up young lovebirds by hand. This is not an easy task, as can be seen from the many young lovebirds that die as a result of an incorrect diet, or way of feeding them. If you want or have to bring up your young lovebirds by hand, you need to take the following into account:

**Agapornis fischeri,** *violet*

*Lovebirds in the nest*

## • Environment

Put the animals in a warm environment, preferably one that is slightly darkened, and not too big. This means the nesting process can be imitated. The temperature must be on the high side for featherless animals, about eighty-six degrees Fahrenheit (thirty degrees Celsius). This can later be brought down. Only after they are about four weeks old, and developing normally, can you offer them the opportunity of coming out of their box every now and then so they can get to know their new environment. Then you can put the nesting box or tray in a cage.

## • Food

Only use specifically prepared food when bringing up lovebird babies by hand. This contains all the necessary ingredients that a baby lovebird needs in the right quantities. Once the animals are old enough to go and explore their new environment, you can offer them solid foods along with their baby food. If everything is going well, you will notice that the bird is eating more and more of the solid food, and less and less of the baby food. Most lovebirds can live off solid foods from the age of 6 to 8 weeks.

• **Don't feed it too much**
Do not feed it more food, or more often, than is stated on the packet. If the packet doesn't give any indication of how much to feed it, you can weigh the animal (for example, using digital scales), and give it approximately 11% of its body weight to eat every day. Do not forget that a baby lovebird grows, and its weight will increase. So the bird must be weighed again every morning. If the bird's crop is not yet empty, do not feed it extra, but wait until it really is empty. This is quite simple to feel. If the crop stays full for too long, seek the advice of a specialist bird veterinarian as soon as possible. It is important to do this because there is a good chance something is wrong. Never force a young bird to eat (more than it wants to eat). The birds themselves often feel fine when their crop is full, but wanting to give more can cause problems for the birds.

**Agapornis personatus,** *dark green pastel*

**• Feeding**
It is best to use a small teaspoon for feeding. Bend the sides so as to form a groove. The idea is to offer the baby food to the baby bird from the spoon, so that it can determine for itself how much to eat.

**• Preventing "snacking on air"**
Try to prevent your bird from swallowing too much air. Make sure the spoon is nice and full.

**• The temperature of the food**
Always make sure the baby food is at the right temperature when feeding, about 100–102 degrees Fahrenheit (38–39 degrees Celsius). Baby food that is too hot can damage the

bird's digestive system, and food that is too cold does not only often taste bad, it can also slow down the digestive process, and that, in turn, can have negative consequences. It is best to check the temperature of the food with a good digital thermometer.

• **No leftovers**
Do not reheat leftovers. Always prepare new baby food.

• **Hygiene**
Clean all used utensils hygienically, by washing them up by hand, or putting them in the dishwasher. Try to spill as little as possible when feeding. If the bird does get dirty, clean it after feeding it, by rubbing it carefully with a lukewarm, damp, cotton cloth (bib, napkin). Never bathe a baby lovebird. The animal does not yet have enough resistance for that.

## • Weighing

Weigh the bird every day. Its weight should increase. If that is not the case, do not wait another day before seeking the advice of a specialist bird veterinarian.

---

Crossbreeding different types

The question of whether different types of lovebirds should be kept pure, or if they can be crossbred, is an ethical one. Many breeders concentrate on consolidating, or introducing new color mutations, within a particular type. And sometimes the fastest way of attaining a new color pattern is through "borrowing" a different type that already has the desired patterning. Others support the idea of keeping types as pure as possible. They only breed natural colors and keep the different types strictly separate. One of the arguments for this is that a pure race of naturally colored animals, that is kept and bred in captivity, can be used as a back up for their own type in the wild, who often don't have it so easy. This has already been done successfully on different occasions with other species of animal–species that have become almost extinct in the wild could be saved, with "new blood" from animal populations kept in captivity.

---

*p. 113:*
*A. nigrigenis–*
*right is an animal*
*deviating from*
*the natural green*
*color*

# 9 ILLNESSES & ABNORMALITIES

## Prevention

It can always happen that a bird becomes sick. The chance of it happening can be greatly reduced, though, by taking preventative measures. Purchasing a bird full of vitality from a reputable source is the first step. Make sure you give it a good and varied diet. Clean the cage hygienically, at least every three or four days. Try and keep stress for the bird(s) to a minimum. Stress results in the body's natural defenses being reduced, causing birds to be more perceptible to illnesses. Make sure that the birds get enough regular exercise and movement, and that there is sufficient ventilation in the room where the bird is kept. Birds that are kept in an aviary have a much greater chance of becoming sick. This is because aviary birds often come into contact with wild birds that can infect them with worms, parasites or other contagious diseases. Moreover, it is more difficult to clean and disinfect than is somewhere indoors. Bacteria therefore find it easier to

*Agapornis personatus, violet multicolored*

multiply, and there are more "hiding places" for parasites.

## The importance of a bird veterinarian.

If you notice that there is something wrong with your bird, there is a good chance that it has been sick for a while. So never wait a couple of days, but take action straight away. If you keep different birds together, separate the bird that does not seem well from the other birds right away. It is usually best if you can go straight to a specialist bird veterinarian. These veterinarians routinely deal with birds, and can recognize symptoms faster because they come across them on a daily basis. They have also often got specialist equipment that a normal veterinarian might not have, because birds are not usually frequent visitors to normal small animals' practices. A bird association will be able to tell you which veterinarians specialize in birds in your local area. If there aren't any bird veterinarians in your area you might have to travel a bit further, but it is often more than worth the extra miles and time.

## Different illnesses

There are many known different kinds of bird diseases and illnesses. The scope of this book does not reach far enough to cover all of them. We limit ourselves here only to the most common diseases and illnesses, as well as some of the most dangerous ones.

## Plucking feathers

Plucking feathers is an undesirable trait that sometimes occurs in lovebirds. The bird can pluck itself, or its partner, bald.
Parents sometimes pluck their young bald. If a lovebird starts plucking, it can be difficult to make it think of anything else. Plucking can occur for different reasons.
• Boredom, that causes this deviant behavior to start
• Loneliness (losing or being apart from a partner)
• Irregular diet
• A skin disorder
• Pain (caused by an internal problem)
• Infection (giardiasis, for example)
• Parasites

There are sprays available to buy that reduce, or temporarily stop, the feather plucking. Even so, it is better not to reach
immediately for the spray, but to first try and work out the
underlying cause, so that it can be eliminated. That's why it
is always a good idea to go to a bird veterinarian if an animal
is plucking itself. If you have several lovebirds together, and
you notice that one or more of the birds has wounds from
feather plucking, separate those birds in question. In doing
so you can prevent more serious consequences–lovebirds can
keep plucking each other so much that it can be fatal, especially if there are already signs of a (bleeding) wound. The
birds in question can eventually be put back together once
they are completely better.

*An* Agapornis taranta *couple*

### External parasites

The most common external parasites in lovebirds are red mites, mange mites, ticks and feather lice. Birds that act as host to (one of) these parasites often become restless. Sometimes the animals eat less than they normally do, and they often lose weight. Parasites in a nest can cause lots of damage. That's why it's very important to make sure that contamination is prevented as much as possible. Making sure the hygiene is good, and that there are no nooks or crannies in the cage, hut, or aviary, where the parasites can flourish, is therefore essential. External parasites can be treated with insecticides that have been specially developed for birds. You can buy these in any well-stocked pet shop or veterinarian's practice.

### Worms (internal parasites)

Worm infections are relatively common in lovebirds. Worms are not as innocent as is often thought. In large num-

**Agapornis nigris,**
*Dark green*

bers especially, they can disrupt the internal organs of a
bird so much that it leads to death. Sometimes a worm
infection can be recognized from traces of blood in the
bird's excrement, and sometimes the bird will (temporarily) also eat noticeably more than normal. But there are
not always such obvious symptoms. Affected birds do
always, though, become thinner. If you think your bird
has got worms, you can get special de-worming treat-
ments from the veterinarian. It is also important to think
of possible re-infection. The excrement from infected
birds is often contaminated with (invisible to us) eggs that
can lead to a new generation of worms. Thorough hygiene
is, especially if there has been the possibility of a worm
infection, absolutely necessary to prevent any repeats of
the disease. Always use a disinfectant that is safe for birds
to clean the homes of the birds that have been infected
with worms.

Some poisonous plants:

Amaryllis
Azalea
Dumbcane *(Dieffenbachia)*
Hyacinth
Mistletoe
Cannabis sativa
Lily of the valley
Iris
Lobelia
Narcissus
Oleander
Aconite
Clematis
Rhododendron
Tobacco
Yew

*A cross between an* A. lilianae *and an* A. fischeri

### Non-stick surfaces

It has been known by bird lovers for quite a while that heating Teflon non-stick surfaces (in pans) lets off gases that can kill a bird, especially those belonging to the parakeet family, fairly quickly. It is not so well-known that this can also be the case with pans made from other materials, non-stick ovens, and grills. Poisonous gases are only usually given off if the temperature of the oven or pan is very hot. But to eliminate all risk it is better not to put your bird in the kitchen, or in a place near a kitchen. There are also known cases where birds nowhere near a kitchen have died nevertheless. It is, therefore, always advisable to be aware.

### Tumors

Occasionally, lovebirds can suffer from tumors. A very fast growing "lump" does not necessarily need to be thought of immediately as a (malignant) tumor. Harmless swellings do sometimes occur. But whether the tumor is malignant or not, it will have to be surgically removed. If you suspect a tumor, it is best to look up a specialist bird veterinarian. Tumors are not always necessarily visible to the eye. Internal tumors can also occur. They can cause a variety of diverse problems, depending on where they are. Internal tumors are often only noticed too late, and this can render them unremovable.

A little cap is
sometimes
(temporarily)
necessary to
prevent the bird
from wounding
itself

### Giardiasis infection

Lovebirds are fairly susceptible to giardiasis infections. The most important symptom of this is feather plucking. It is also nearly always the case that weight loss, diarrhea, loss of appetite, and flaky or scaly skin can occur. If you suspect that your lovebird is infected with giardiasis, you can examine some of your bird's excrement to see if it really is present. Medicines are available, but unfortunately it seems that giardiasis infections are very difficult to get under control, as they are so resistant.

### Newcastle disease NCD

Newcastle disease is a virus to which different types of birds, including lovebirds, are susceptible. The symptoms can be very diverse. The most common ones are difficulty with breathing, and watery diarrhea, but the illness can also sometimes cause cold like symptoms or isolated lameness. Affected animals usually lose their appetites and eat little or nothing. Animals that have the disease usually die between six to nine days after showing the first symptoms. It is only possible to find out if a bird really did die from

*Symptoms of sickness should never be underestimated: make sure you bring in a good specialist bird veterinarian*

Newcastle disease retrospectively with a laboratory test. There are antigens available that protect the birds against this illness. But they only work for a few months. In practice, these antigens are only given if the disease is in a certain area.

## Bird tuberculosis

Bird tuberculosis is one of the most feared bird illnesses. Luckily it is not too common, relatively speaking. It is, in fact, taken so seriously because of the risk of it being passed over to people. The disease is caused by a bacterium, the Mycobacterium avium. The spreading and infection of this bacterium can be caused by breathing, but also from picking up foods that carry the bacteria, or infected drinking water. The danger with this disease is that symptoms often only begin to appear later on in the illness. The animals become thinner and often suffer from diarrhea. It is very difficult to figure out if a bird has got bird tuberculosis, because there doesn't appear to be any watertight way of confirming it. An autopsy after the bird has died can prove it conclusively, because it can be seen that the liver and

spleen have been affected. Unfortunately, there is no reme-
dy for this illness. And birds are, in any case, not the only
carriers of the M. avium. Research has shown that pigs can
also be carriers of the bacteria.

### Parrot illnesses (psittacosis/chlamydiosis)

The parrot disease, also known as the bird disease (orni-
thosis), is caused by Chlamydia psicatti. The cause of this
disease can spread itself in a variety of different ways–it
can be spread through the air, but also by water, food,
other objects, and external parasites. It is so greatly feared
because it is also infectious for people–a so-called zoono-
sis. Lovebirds infected with the parrot disease can show
several diverse symptoms. The excrement is often thin,
green in color, and mixed with traces of blood. The affected bird is apathetic, appears to have a cold (weeping from
the nose and eyes, sneezing), and sometimes has difficulty
breathing. The treacherousness of this disease is that sick
animals can infect other birds, and people as well, without

*If your bird
scratches itself
a lot, it could
be suffering
from parasites*

showing any symptoms of the disease. It is possible to test excrement in a laboratory, to see if there really are traces of this disease. Luckily, there are medicines available that can cure the parrot disease. People who have caught this disease do not necessarily, just as is the case with birds, need to become ill. The disease usually manifests itself in people who do not have much resistance. They will then get complaints similar to those found with lung infections, or the flu, where normal medicines do not really cure the problems. Luckily, the chance that your bird has, or will get, this disease, is much reduced if hygiene is taken seriously. It is important to be aware of the possible symptoms, nevertheless.

## Psittacine beak and feather disease (PBFD)
The beak and feather disease is a very infectious disease that mainly occurs in (young) parrot–like birds, and is caused by

a virus. The recognizable characteristic of this disease is a defection with the feathers, usually with the large flight feathers, and the beak. The bird can look very scruffy, and be partially bald. The disease causes diminished resistance, so the affected animal could eventually die from secondary infections that it would normally be able to protect itself from. Just as is the case with other diseases, it is possible for birds affected by the beak and feather disease to not show any symptoms. Such animals can, however, still spread the disease. This happens, with beak and feather disease, via droppings or flakes of skin. The disease can be confirmed by means of a blood test, but this possibility is as yet confined to only a small number of laboratories. There are no

**Agapornis personatus,** *mauve colored*

*A feather from a bird suffering from beak and feather disease*

medicines available that will cure the beak and feather disease. Vaccines against it are, however, being developed.

# 10 Addresses

**Lovebird Society (UK)**
76 The Cheslis
Stivichall, Coventry CV3 5BL
United Kingdom

**North American Parrot Society, Inc.**
P.O. Box 404
Salem, OH 44460

**The Parrot Association of Canada**
637316 St. Vincent Township, R.R. #1
Meaford, ON  N4L 1W5

**Parrot Society of Australia Inc**
P.O. Box 75
Salisbury, Queensland 4107
Australia

**African Lovebird Society**
Box 142
San Marcos, CA 92069

# 11 PHOTOGRAPH ACKNOWLEDGEMENTS

**Pieter van den Hooven:**
pages 7-17, 18 right, 21, 23, 24 above, 25, 27 below, 29, 30, 32 above, 33 below, 37, 38 above, 41, 44-52, 53 left, 54, 55 below, 57, 65, 66, 69, 71, 73, 79, 81-87, 88 above, 91, 92, 98-106, 108-110, 113-119, 123, 124.

**Loes de Jong:**
pages 40 below, 62.

**Ellen Uittenbogaard:**
pages 19, 22, 24 below, 26, 27 above, 32 below, 90, 40 above, 43, 53 right, 56, 58, 61, 63, 64, 67, 68, 70, 72, 75, 80, 93, 95, 96, 97 below, 107, 112-122, 125.

**Esther Verhoef:**
pages 18 left, 31, 33 above, 36, 42, 55 above, 60, 74, 76 t/m 78, 88 below, 89, 90, 97 above.

**Angelique van Voorst:**
pages 20, 28, 38 below.

**Renate Hagenouw:**
page 59.